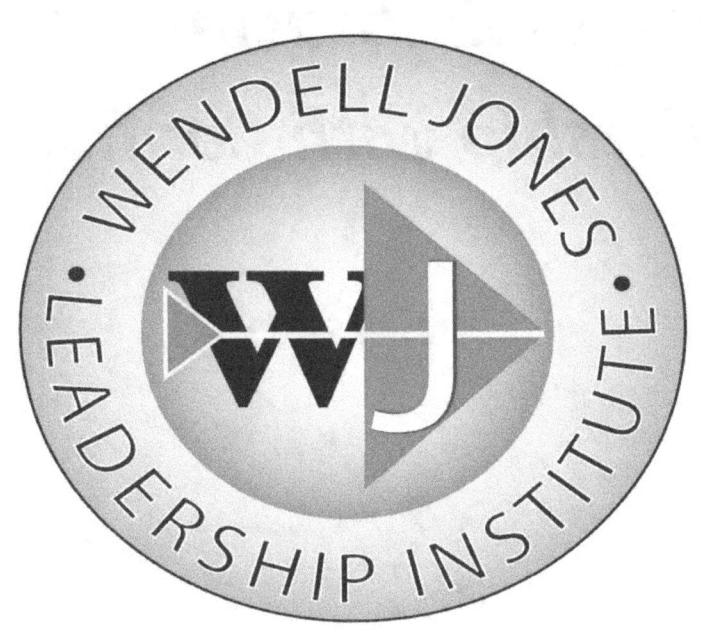

Women in Leadership:
Excelling in a Man's World Workbook
Your Guide to Embracing Your Call to Leadership with Confidence

Table of Contents

Introduction ……………………………………………………………………………………………….page 4

Women Leaders: Unique, Effective and Needed …………………………………………….....page 6

Be Your Whole Entire Self ………………………………………………………………………….page 11

Doing a Great Job is Simply Not Enough ……………………………………………………….page 16

It's All About Positioning: Building Credibility and Increasing Your Visibility ……………..page 22

Communication: A Key to Leadership Success ……………………………………………….page 30

Turn Challenges into Opportunities. Addressing Today's Challenges …………………….page 35

I Wish I Had Known ………………………………………………………………………………..page 39

Call to Leadership ………………………………………………………………………………….page 42

The Women In Leadership: Excelling in a Man's World Introduction
"To have the future we all want, women must help in leading the way"

Inspiration, it's all around us. There is rarely a moment that goes by without someone trying to persuade, inspire, or motivate us to do something; usually an image or lifestyle that we're encouraged to duplicate. When it comes to defining who you are and what you stand for, who inspires you? In thinking about you, does being a leader come to mind? Have you ever been presented with the image of leadership and persuaded to follow that path? Was the image that of a woman?

Growing up I was surrounded by strong-willed, hardworking women whose leadership upheld the traditions and values of our family. My grandmothers, neighborhood moms, mother, and aunts all possessed natural leadership skills that made them the masters of being well-organized, industrious, courageous, and resourceful- doing what had to be done and wasting nothing. However, when I was a younger professional who was just joining the workforce, not seeing women in leadership positions felt detrimental to my identity and what I had always known and seen- women leading. I aspired to be more professionally, but I saw few, if any, images of women leaders to model myself after. If there wasn't a place for professional, purpose-filled women leaders who had wisdom and skills to share, how could I ever attempt to do the same?

Women, we have put in a lot of work to get where we are, but many of us continue to struggle to be recognized as the smart and equally capable leaders that we are. Despite some success, many of us still doubt our own abilities and see ourselves as less effective than our counterparts. Many times, I have felt like there wasn't a place for me in leadership, but there is—even if it wasn't clear at that particular time, and there continues to be a place for someone like me and for someone like you. Women, your leadership matters and there's a

> *Many times, I have felt like there wasn't a place for me in leadership, but there is—even if it wasn't clear at that particular time, and there continues to be a place for someone like me and for someone like you.*

place for all of us to lead. The Women in Leadership: Excelling in a Man's World will uncover how to embrace your call to leadership and unleash your God-given gifts, skills, and experiences to make an even greater impact to the world. Your application of the learnings will help you in going from potential to demonstrated ability. You will also receive road-tested principles, not theories, and you will gain a clear understanding of who you are and why your being at the table means more progress for us all.

Through this encouraging environment let's do these four things: (1) compare notes with your peers, (2) deepen your understanding of the practices of successful women leaders, (3) utilize each class as a powerful networking tool as women come together to recognize their shared leadership strengths, and lastly (4) work together to overcome barriers to advancement. I'm eager to see you take off the cap to your own leadership capacity and increase your ability to influence the world around you.

Women, let's inspire. Let's be an example. Women, it's time to lead.

Women In Leadership: Excelling in a Man's World

Lesson 1: Women Leaders: Unique, Effective, and Needed

"Being a confident woman is not acting like a man." Lisa Bevere

It bears repeating, growing up I was always surrounded by strong-willed, hardworking women. These leaders were successful in managing the divergent demands for their attention: managing the household, working full-time, helping with homework, monitoring the neighborhood to keep everyone's child on the straight and narrow, and most importantly, ensuring the "candy lady" was in place to run the candy store out of her kitchen window so that the sugar-feigning children could see how far $0.50 would take them. These awesome women put out fires, managed crisis and change, and they kept everyone in check while running the household. These great women influenced my development and how I socialized and evolved. Through my bird's eye view of their leadership, they instilled in me the passion to commit to and to strive for success. I had no other choice.

Leaders are powerful. I saw this in the women I grew up with; I experienced it. Leaders are the best sowers of opportunities right in front of them. Yes, my mom could make a meal out of what appeared to be nothing and feed a family of 5 with leftovers to spare. Leaders aren't self-made; they are driven. I can't recall a spring, summer, or fall that the "candy lady" didn't drive herself to open her kitchen window to sell the best Kool-Aid "flip-flops"/icees. Leaders have guts to confront issues, no matter how unpopular it makes them; even if that means the neighborhood mom calling your parents at work because you refuse to follow the "stay in the house until mom and dad get home" rules. Leadership pays and invests. The "candy lady" increased her income and the mothers of the neighborhood produced future leaders.

Who were some of the first women leaders that made an impression on you and how did they help you to see yourself?

_____
_____
_____
_____

As a young professional who was just joining the workforce, not seeing women in leadership positions felt detrimental to my identity and what I had always known and seen; women leading. I aspired to be more professionally, but I saw few, if any, images of women leaders to model myself after. I was hopeful that I would see the likes of the women leaders that I had always known growing up: gutsy, authentic, industrious, confident, and experienced. I was searching, from role to role, but no luck. If there wasn't a place for professional, purpose-filled women leaders who had wisdom and skills to share, how could I ever attempt to do the same? We have seen the effects of positive role modeling. We learn how to respond, adapt, behave, feel, and yes, lead. Women need images, visible demonstrations of strong women in leadership roles to broaden the conversation and transform the way we see ourselves. "If she can see it, she can be it." Women are needed.

What women have helped you to see yourself positively different and how?

_____
_____
_____
_____

As more women embrace their call to leadership it is important that everyone works to provide encouragement, resources, and a demonstration to help them *see* and attain equity, advancements in the workplace, and leadership tools for their tool belt. Why? Despite gains in every business and profession, women are underrepresented at all levels of leadership. Women's underrepresentation in leadership has been framed as a deficit in which something is holding women back from becoming leaders- the glass ceiling. I'm sure you've heard of the term glass ceiling, the symbolic, invisible wall that high-achieving women hit that prevents them from rising beyond a certain level. So if women in leadership are underrepresented due to the 'glass ceiling', who is overrepresented due to a 'glass escalator?' Men.

Do the qualities of leadership differ between men and women? There are individual differences and gender differences, but should the eligibility conditions of a woman leader be based on her body parts? Women and men are not the same and that's a great thing, something that should be celebrated, however it's been abused.

Why would there be a difference in the way men and women lead? What does sex have to do with it? Why is it that when a woman leader exhibits leadership behaviors she is perceived more negatively than a man with the same behaviors? The impact of stereotypes. Often, women are called aggressive instead of proactive. We are identified as being fixated versus laser-focused. In addition to that, women are told to "man up" or "grow a pair" as if leadership is masculine. Here is the issue. Communicating that a woman must act "like a man" and "man up" not only implies that acting "like a woman" is not as effective, but also reinforces the notion that being assertive is not something women do.

> *Communicating that a woman must act "like a man" and "man up" not only implies that acting "like a woman" is not as effective, but also reinforces the notion that being assertive is not something women do.*

Betty White said so eloquently, "Why do they always tell you to grow a pair of balls? Balls are weak and sensitive. Why don't they tell you to grow a vagina? Those things really take a pounding!" The language and gestures of power presupposes that men are innately tougher and likely to be more successful than women. Example. If I order steak and my boyfriend orders fish or if he orders wine and I get a beer and the waiter is left to decide between us, I always seemingly receive the "weaker" option.

Brainstorm on gestures, words and phrases you have seen, said, and/or heard, that reveal stereotypical "male" traits?

_____
_____
_____
_____

Women faint; men pass out. She's aggressive; he's assertive. She's too tough while he's determined. Women are testy; men are edgy. Am I missing something? While male leaders are allowed to have complex personalities, powerful women are often summed up by stereotypes that undermine them and their power.

What is your least favorite stereotype about powerful women?

_____
_____
_____

Let's take a moment to examine how women have been asked to survive and thrive in the often-male dominated worlds.

Brainstorm on gestures, words and phrases you have seen, said, and/or heard that reveals stereotypical 'female' traits?

_____
_____
_____
_____

Which traits do you believe serve women best? Which traits do you believe hold women back?

_____
_____
_____
_____

Disrupting the stereotypical use of language should always be our goal.

How can women get past stereotypes and rise to leadership roles? Try these tips:

1. _____
2. _____
3. _____
4. _____

What will you apply immediately?

_____
_____
_____
_____
_____
_____

Women In Leadership: Excelling in a Man's World
Lesson 2: Be Your Whole Entire Self

"You will find that achievement will not fulfill you, but the discovery into your own purpose will."

The role you play at work is only a small part of who you are, and for some, when we arrive to work it's under the guise of another persona. Have you been made to feel that you need to be one person at work and another person at home? As an African-American professional, who loves the skin I'm in, I've at times felt pressured to conform – real or perceived- causing inclusion efforts in the workplace to stall, if they were moving at all. I would work extremely hard to not be seen associating with other African-American professionals at certain events in order to avoid being seen as a "clique." I've also felt some discomfort about wearing my natural hair, so I only did so on the weekends. These pressures can easily place individuals on silos. There was a fascinating study by Deloitte that found that more than half of us cover up part of our identity at work to try to fit in. The 'half ' that the Deloitte study speaks of revealed that these multiple personas disproportionally impact those who are historically underrepresented in the workforce (i.e. women, women of color, minorities, and the LGBT community). Let's talk about it.

Have you or someone that you know ever felt pressured to downplay your identity in a way that your counterparts did not? Let's hear about it.

_____
_____
_____
_____

The Deloitte study reveals that identity "covering" has occurred in greater frequency within groups that have been historically underrepresented. Why do you think that is?

_____
_____
_____
_____

To what degree do you believe identity covering impacted your/others sense of opportunity/advancement within the organization and your/their commitment to it?

_____
_____
_____
_____

Purpose; failing to fully know who you are will have you falling prey to covering your identity and lessening the impact you are called to make for the benefit of others. Each of us can and **will** uncover our purpose and bring it fully to our respective organizations, employers, and to our lives.

Understanding our identity in Christ gives us purpose, Hannah Anderson, author of *Made for More*, explained, "As women made in the image of God, we must be productive, life-giving people because our God is a productive, life-giving God." If we want to understand our identity as women, we must first understand His identity as God.

Women, being made in the image of God means we must be engaged in meaningful work. Becoming a leader involves much more than being put in a leadership role, acquiring new skills, and adapting one's style to the requirements of that role. It involves a fundamental identity shift away from the stereotypes.

Your personal identity is rooted in the way that God sees you. Your identity should be very important to you because it will affect the way you feel about yourself, how and if you give God glory, and how you behave in challenging situations.

Knowing your identity is in Christ is one thing, but understanding it and applying this truth will practically change the way you live and lead. A revealing activity is to complete the sentence "I am ____." The answers given disclose where a person gains identity. The identities we assign ourselves powerfully influence our direction and decisions in life. So, who are you?

> *Knowing your identity is in Christ is one thing, but understanding it and applying this truth will practically change the way you live and lead.*

I am…

_____
_____
_____
_____

What do people seek you out for?
_____
_____
_____
_____

Who are you drawn to help?
_____
_____
_____
_____

As you reflect on some of your peak experiences throughout your career and personal life, when do you experience the greatest sense of "aliveness?"
_____
_____
_____
_____

What is the lasting impact you want to leave in your current assignment and/or your life as a leader?
_____
_____
_____
_____

Women, do not become conditioned to boundaries because of your gender. Your identity and your purpose are about who you are in God. God did not choose to use women because there

were no men available. Women as leaders was apart of God's plan from the very beginning. Exercising leadership and being a good steward of our work is part of what it means for humans to be created in the image of God. Today is the day you can begin living like the woman God designed you to be. You are a kingdom woman, which means you make a difference wherever you are planted. Be encouraged to be transformed by God's truth of who you are.

As a leader, dimming your light is not allowed. If you are a great leader, and you are, you must shine light a city on a hill! Lead with confidence because of who God says you are and what you can do through Him. There is a growing body of evidence that shows just how devastating this lack of confidence can be. Success, as it turns out, correlates just as closely with confidence as it does with competence.

What has your lack of confidence talked you out of doing or made you believe about yourself?

_____
_____
_____
_____

Be your whole entire self. The next generation of leaders look up to you now and want to know how you do what you do. They also need to see who you are when you're not in "work mode." How do you balance work, family, time for yourself, and friends? How do you respond when you're stressed? How do you take care of yourself? What does your marriage look like? Who are your closest friends, and how do you support one another? What are you thinking?

_____
_____
_____
_____
_____
_____
_____

Your greatest demonstration of being a leader doesn't come from the desk, the job, or the platform. It comes when others witness the thousands of everyday moments when the character of Christ is being formed in you. Allow other young women to see your *real* life. They don't just need to learn leadership skills; they need to develop the character that supports the work God wants to do in and through them. Be your whole entire self and invite them into your world. Provide them with an inside look into how God is at work in your everyday, chaotic life. What will you apply immediately?

_____
_____
_____
_____
_____
_____
_____
_____
_____
_____
_____
_____
_____
_____
_____
_____
_____
_____
_____
_____

Women In Leadership: Excelling in a Man's World

Lesson 3: Doing A Great Job is Simply Not Enough

Do you have an assignment that needs to be completed and completed with accuracy? Call April, she will get it done with no complaints. It will be turned in on time and with more insight than what you asked for. Quick question for you. Do you have an assignment that needs to be completed and completed with accuracy? Delegate the work to April. She will get it done with no complaints, turned in on time, and with more insight than what you asked for. I could continue to repeat this because I was the "go-to queen." I didn't take risks, I just wanted to do a good job and keep my head down- show some good ole humility. I was going nowhere fast within the company and here's why. I was a glorified office facilitator. I didn't position myself to be a strategist, visionary, or someone who contributed to the end-to-end process. I was task-oriented but not vision-driven. I was expressive but I wasn't a communicator. My goal was always a 'Perfect 10," but I failed to look for a win – win where agendas aligned. I was wading in my own comfort zone as I was shooting myself in the foot!

There are four zones we can fall into:

Blah Zone

_____
_____
_____
_____
_____

Comfort Zone

_____
_____
_____
_____

Stretch Zone

Yikes Zone

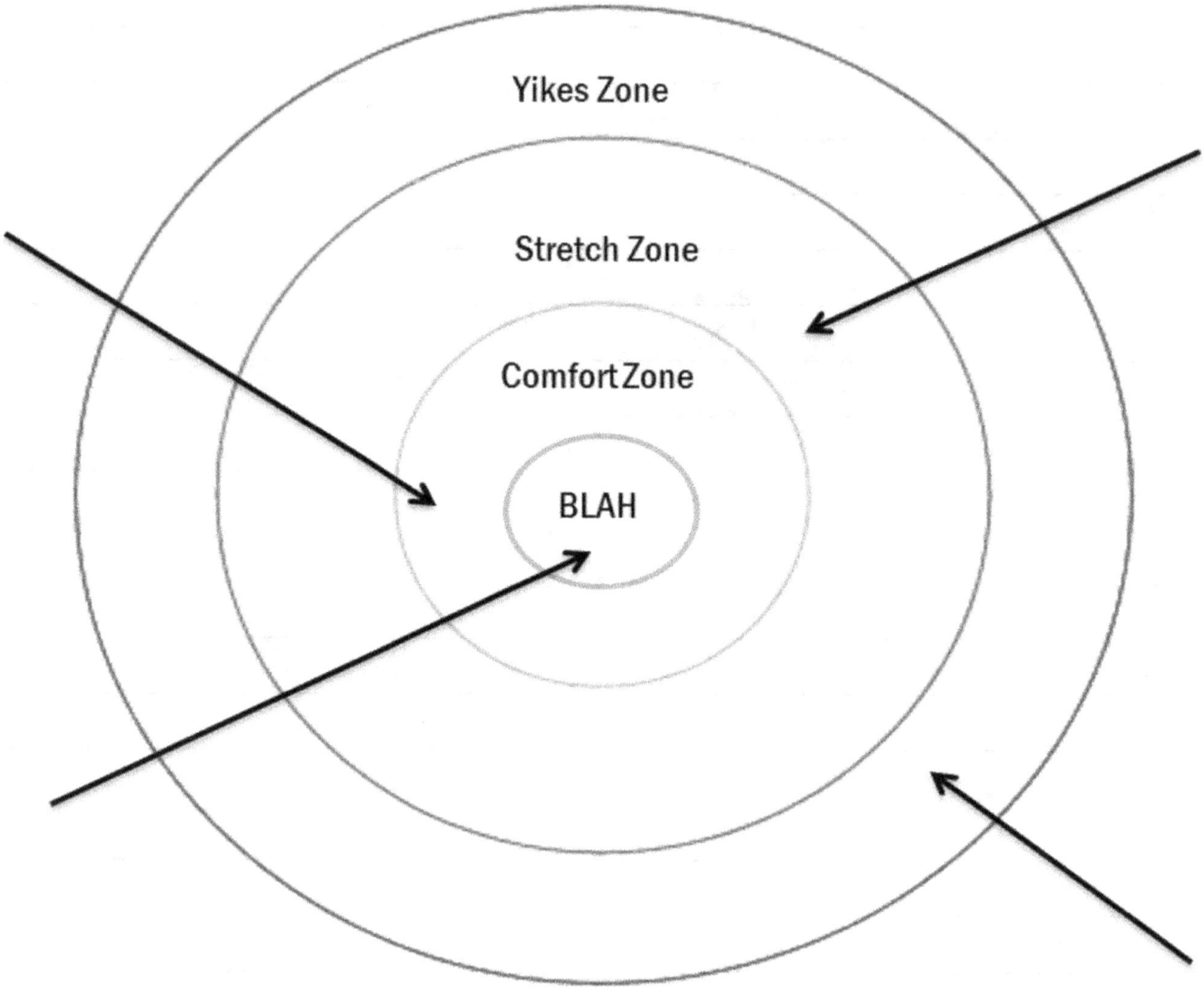

Yikes Zone

Stretch Zone

Comfort Zone

BLAH

In which zone does the most learning occur and why?

_____
_____
_____
_____
_____
_____

Which zone are you generally in? _____

One comment I've heard a lot is, "I wish I had your confidence." It is so humbling to me that people are inspired by my ability to communicate, whether teaching or training, but I want to be clear: anyone has the ability to challenge themselves and increase their sense of their own worth and abilities. You can be the confident woman that you want to be, and you can do it while being scared!

Do it scared. Fear coexists with confidence.

My Pastor, Wendell Jones, always teaches, "Do it scared. Fear coexists with confidence." So what do you do? Apply the teaching of course and do it scared!

What is fear?

F: _____

E: _____

A: _____

R: _____

Name 3 fears that you have faced as a leader that has kept you in the Comfort Zone?

1. _____.
2. _____.
3. _____.

How will you move past the fear?

_____
_____
_____
_____
_____
_____
_____
_____

There are four common fears that prevent leaders from moving beyond the Blah and Comfort Zones. Let's confront them with solutions.

1. Criticism	
2. Failure	
3. Making Decisions	
4. Responsibility	

If you allow fear to paralyze you, your world will become a place where you no longer want to be. You will want out of the very place you were born to make an impact. Like me, you have to choose to keep going and to keep doing, all while being aware of your triggers as you're stretching.

Know your triggers and identify stretching.

What are your triggers?

_____

_____

_____

What is stretching?

_____

_____

_____

Stretch assignments, what are they and how do you get them?

_____
_____
_____
_____

What will you apply immediately?

_____
_____
_____
_____
_____
_____
_____
_____
_____
_____
_____
_____
_____
_____
_____
_____
_____

Women In Leadership: Excelling in a Man's World
Lesson 4: It's All About Positioning: Building Credibility and Increasing Your Visibility

"Even if you're on the right track, you'll get run over if you just sit there." – Will Rogers

Some women mistakenly believe that their performance at work is the most important factor in moving up the ladder. Most women come in and get the job done and take on additional assignments because they were asked- in addition to accomplishing their tasks. Many women leaders are strongly task-focused, display much confidence towards their work, and their knowledge and leadership has earned the respect of the team. They hope that their actions and work performance will replace having to engage/speak to upper management about future opportunities. Most believe that if they continue giving "work" their all and getting good results, someone will eventually notice and promote them, right? Not necessarily. I like to call these types the *'quietly, amazing leader.'* These individuals are under the radar, running a stealth operation of greatness that's impacting the success of the business, yet being positioned to boost your success in the workplace is not as simple as just sitting at your desk.

Silence is golden, but here, the squeaky wheel gets the oil.

You have the right to remain silent, but if you don't toot your own horn there is no music. Many women respond with silence instead of participating and sharing their insights in meetings, voicing their opinions, or even asking for challenging projects or assignments to gain more exposure. Where do you believe this origin of this silence comes from?

_____
_____
_____
_____

Waiting Game

All good things come to those who wait. But time and tide wait for no man.

Does waiting in line, waiting to be called upon, make you a better person? _____

Why do we wait "our turn?" Could it be possible that some of us secretly enjoy waiting in line because we will not be challenged to step out of our comfort zones, new learning is not required (placing us back in a position of vulnerability), and of course, no new responsibilities to be accountable for? What do you think?

_____
_____
_____
_____

I agree that waiting is a part of life, but often time we CHOOSE to wait or persuade ourselves that we have to wait. We tell ourselves that we can't take action or move forward for a number of reasons, and trust me, no one could *out wait* me! If there were no line, I created one. Complete these "Once/Then" statements

Once _____ happens, then I will _____
_____.

Once I feel _____ then I will _____
_____.

Is there still a need for you to wait based on your "Once/Then" statements? Explain.

_____
_____
_____
_____

When you get into a line, you're not fully accounting for the fact that you are slowing down everybody who arrives after you- other girls, young ladies, and women. Once again,

> *When we wait for others to do something, we give them control; no one should control your narrative but you.*

you're taking an action that does not account for the cost you're imposing on other people. When we wait for others to do something, we give them control; no one should control your narrative but you. While we consciously decide to wait, we withhold our contribution to the

world, and the world desperately needs the contribution that each of us has to give. Instead of waiting, we should just START!

Executive Presence

Do you have it? Can you command a room? Do people stop and listen when you speak? If so, you have likely mastered the art of "executive presence". Executive presence begins with how we see ourselves from the inside out, how we wish to be seen and thought of, and how we build perception.

What is executive presence and why is it important?

_____
_____
_____
_____

Three-dimensional Executive Presence Model

Character

_____
_____
_____

Substance

_____
_____
_____

Style

_____
_____
_____

Executive Presence Model		
Character	**Substance**	**Style**
A	P	A
I	C	I
C	C	I
R	R	I
H	V	A

~credit given to the Bates ExPI Executive Presence Model

It's important to clarify that measuring executive presence isn't about whether the leader has these qualities. It's about whether these qualities are showing up in the leader's communication and interactions with key stakeholders.

Visibility

Are you asking yourself the question, "How do I increase visibility?" If you're not, you should be. It's never safe to assume that decision-makers are aware of your accomplishments. Don't allow a quiet nature and somewhat passive approach to interfere with your need to be visible. Future opportunities and other influential people may not be aware of your value. Increasing your visibility doesn't require constant bragging and acting life you are self-promoting, but you do need to stand out and get noticed.

So how do you judge if you're visible enough or not? Great question! Here are three warning signs to help you determine whether you need to work on being more visible:

Warning #1 _____
_____
_____
_____

Warning #2 _____
_____
_____
_____

Warning #3 _____

_____
_____
_____

There are many ways to increase your visibility without being overbearing.

Seek out _____

_____
_____
_____

Leverage _____ _____

_____
_____
_____

Gain _____ _____

_____
_____
_____

Speak _____ and _____

_____
_____
_____

Master_____

_____
_____

Volunteer_____

_____
_____

Schedule_____

_____

_____

Become visible *now*. Don't wait to feel comfortable. Take action now by selecting at least two ideas from the above list and implementing them over the next two weeks.

What two ideas will you implement?

_____

_____

_____

_____

Networking

"As iron sharpens iron, so a friend sharpens a friend." – Proverbs 27:17NLT King Solomon's writings are filled with illustrations that demonstrate the power of meaningful relationships. He believed good friends could sharpen one another—that "metal to metal" relationships would result in an improved life. He also believed that poor relationships would wound us. Ultimately, he claimed, we are the product of our friendships, whether good or bad. The king clearly understood that human beings were never made to "go it alone." He taught us that God often uses the influences of others to shape and prepare our destinies. We can never be all God intended for us to be without significant people in our lives. King Solomon's words tell us that a quality friend will offer valuable counsel: "The heartfelt counsel of a friend is as sweet as perfume and incense" (27:9). Literally, this means a real friend will give "fit"—that is, timely and appropriate—advice (see 15:23). Successful networking is all about building intimate, sincere relationships based on mutual generosity, not duplicity. God never intended for any of us to do life alone, therefore, don't discount the value in networking.

Networking is based on the question "_____"

and not "_____."

Networking Defined

_____
_____
_____

The time to build relationships is *before* you need to start a job search or before you are ready to change positions. Putting off networking limits opportunities both internally and externally. Sheryl Sandberg, COO of Facebook, says, "Women are missing an opportunity. Networking not only expands business opportunities within company walls and externally. It creates that space where professional boundaries are softened by personality, often paving the way for women to be more effective in driving initiatives forward in the workplace. It allows women to find role models and business leads not available inside their office. Most important, social connection and professional engagement is what makes our jobs interesting and enduring."

Leadership today is increasingly defined not just by how many hours you spend at your computer, but your ability to connect to others, how you incorporate outside perspectives, and how you navigate groups. Networking takes time, but it matters. The importance of confidence and connections are key opportunities to influence a woman's perceptions of leadership.

> *Leadership today is increasingly defined not just by how many hours you spend at your computer, but your ability to connect to others*

What will you apply immediately?
_____
_____
_____
_____
_____
_____

Women In Leadership: Excelling in a Man's World
Lesson 5: Communication: A Key to Leadership Success

"The single biggest problem in communication is the illusion that it has taken place."
(George Bernard Shaw)

If it could all be so simple- communication. I hear this all the time, "Say what you mean!" Well, I did say what I meant but by the time the message got to you, it was lost in translation. Frustrating right? Tiring, to say the least. Communication is about more than just exchanging information. It's about understanding the emotion and intentions behind the information. Women, it is simply impossible to become a great leader without being a great communicator; notice that I did not refer to being a great talker. It doesn't matter what you know about anything if you can't communicate. In that event, you are not even a failure; you're just not there.

Far too many times we are taught to focus on ourselves to be an effective communicator. We are trained to focus on vocabulary, presence, delivery, grammar, etc. These things are important to learn, but if you want better communication results, zoom in on the elements that focus on others. Remember, *the message is not about the messenger*; it has nothing to do with messenger; it is however 100% about meeting the needs and the expectations of those you're communicating with.

When you examine some of the world's greatest leaders you'll find them to be exceptional communicators. Let's take a moment to name a few leaders who you believe possess exceptional communication skills:

_____   _____   _____

What makes these leaders champions of effective communication?

_____

_____

_____

_____

Call it credibility. Call it personal power. Whatever you call it, communication is critical to your success.

What are your top five toughest communication situations?

1. _____
2. _____
3. _____
4. _____
5. _____

We communicate the way we do because of how we were taught to communicate. How we communicate with the world has been influenced by who we are, our backgrounds, our education, our values and beliefs, our needs, positions, jobs, and more. What were your early examples of how to communicate communication as a child?

_____

_____

_____

_____

Everything a leader says will be interpreted. Everything. Every word that a leader uses matters and must be chosen wisely. Make sure that your communication is crystal clear and direct. You have to paint a crisp picture of your vision, challenge or solution in order for the team to rally behind it and help you make it happen.

As a leader, name three things that can be accomplished through effective communication?

1. _____
2. _____
3. _____

The problem arises when what you say and how you say it can lead to misunderstandings and misinterpretations, which can ultimately disrupt your progress, teamwork, or derail your goal for upward mobility.

The ability to think on one's feet, organize one's thoughts and articulate them is critical. Communicating effectively is one of the most valuable assets any job seeker can possess in terms of career advancement and long-term career success. Not having it, on the other hand, can be like an anchor dragging an otherwise competent individual into a career of mediocrity.

Communicate Effectively

Now, let's focus on you! How well do you express yourself? Can you articulate your thoughts and ideas clearly? Developing the appropriate vocabulary to adequately describe your thoughts and ideas is a skill that sets many apart, but when these skills are either not developed or not practiced, they can diminish over time, reducing your ability to adequately and accurately convey your thoughts and meaning.

Speaking effectively means being able to understand what you want to say and having a vocab developed enough so you are able to have those receiving your message understand it clearly and as intended.

Many of the thousands of words you know were learned whether you worked at it or not. How did this learning occur?

_____
_____
_____

Let's be intentional. There are several ways to improve your vocabulary. Let's explore them.

_____
_____
_____

Communicate the Why

What does the "WHY" do?

_____
_____

_____

_____

Believe it or not, all communication is personal. People will take your message and interpret, analyze, and amplify it in terms of their experience.

The Three C's to Communication

1. 1st C _____
2. 2nd C_____
3. 3rd C_____

When leaders communicate, they do so with the following three goals in mind:

1. _____

_____
_____
_____
_____

2. _____

_____
_____
_____
_____

3. _____

_____
_____
_____
_____

So what's the moral? Do whatever it takes to become an effective communicator. It's definitely worth the effort.

Believe it or not, all communication is personal. People will take your message and interpret, analyze, and amplify it in terms of their experience.

What will you apply immediately?

Women In Leadership: Excelling in a Man's World

Lesson 6: Turn Challenges into Opportunities. Addressing today's Challenges

To get a successful outcome you can't consider failure as an option. Together we will address today's challenges and the most effective tools in overcoming these challenges. Here's why. Women and men are not having the same experiences at work. Women get less access to the people and opportunities that advance careers and are disadvantaged in many of their daily interactions. Women are also less than half as likely as men to say they see a lot of people like them in senior management, and they're right—only one in five senior executives is a woman. What's a woman to do? Turn challenges into opportunities of course!

Negotiation

Most of us don't negotiate—with our bosses, our clients, even our cable companies. Why? We know we're leaving money on the table, but we're not sure what to say. We don't want it to be awkward. And what if they say no?

The negotiation process revolves around two factors: what you are worth and what they are willing to pay for you.

Guess what follows you to your next job? Your current salary. Do you really want your *current salary* to follow you? Our first challenge that we will address is pay.

Let's discuss three reasons why you should negotiate your salary.

1._____

_____

2._____

_____

3._____

_____

Common Negotiation Mistakes Women Make

1._____

_____

2._____

_____

3._____
_____

Negotiation Tactics

1._____
_____

2._____
_____

3._____
_____

4._____
_____

5._____
_____

Double Minority or Double Jeopardy

Gender and racial stereotypes overlap to create unique—and uniquely powerful—stereotypes. According to one recent study, races are perceived as gendered, with being black considered more masculine than being white, and being Asian considered more feminine than being white. While being great at your job, woman of color, I wonder if you overcompensate by trying to prove your value and yourself. Do you second-guess decisions you normally might not have? Do you feel the pressure is on to represent for the educated minority woman?

What are your least favorite parts about the racial divide in leadership?

_____
_____
_____
_____

There are just some things that school/ college, and life experiences just don't prepare you for. It can prep you for what and what not to say during an interview. It can give you career training and knowledge of your field of study, but the one thing, however, that school/college fails to prepare many of us for is what we will encounter once we're actually hired. The American Dream leads us to believe that hard work and dedication are all that you need to succeed in this country; however, they fail to disclose the little disclaimer that says, "Please Note: This dream is often only applicable to qualifying races." Leader, do not be sorry or make any apologies for who you are and refuse to be broken. How can you overcome prevailing attitudes about women of color to be successful?

Leader, do not be sorry or make any apologies for who you are and refuse to be broken.

_____
_____
_____
_____

Leadership Socialization

Childhood lessons and early exposure to leadership have a significant impact on a woman's perceptions of her ability to lead. Your views of leadership begin to take shape early in childhood, starting with the values you learn, your exposure to leadership skills, and whether you have leadership role models. Were you encouraged to lead as a child or were you taught to be nice to others? Did you have a role model or was anyone intentional in your development as a young leader? Factors such as these become significant milestones in the aspiring leader's life.

How were you socialized to leadership growing up?

_____
_____
_____
_____

What will you apply immediately?

Women in Leadership: Excelling in a Man's World
Lesson 7: I Wish I Had Known

There are lessons you learned growing up that are still influencing you as a woman today. These lessons may not all be helpful to your now. Creating an environment where you can thrive begins with you and what you know. We will do deep dives into several topics to identify actions that will contribute to women achieving their potential.

Stay True to You

_____
_____
_____
_____

Stay Open to Opportunities or Create Them

_____
_____
_____
_____

Leadership is All About Adaptability

_____
_____
_____
_____

The Importance of A Mentor and Sponsor

_____
_____
_____
_____
_____
_____

Resource Planning/Pipeline Conversations

___

Be Constantly Learning

___

Any other suggestions?

___

What will you apply immediately?

___

Women in Leadership: Excelling in a Man's World
Lesson 8: Call to Action

Leadership is the job of all women who seek better outcomes and aspire for greatness. It is our responsibility to contribute and lead up and lead down. Women, we benefit economies, social development, communities, and families. Move forward and apply what you have learned. "Women in Leadership: Excelling in a Man's World" sessions have been an urge for you to take up the challenge of leading in application. With all steps taken to apply what you have received in each session, you will improve your prospects, livelihoods and their yields.

Panel Discussion Notes

_____
_____
_____
_____
_____
_____
_____
_____
_____
_____
_____
_____
_____
_____
_____
_____
_____
_____
_____
_____

www.ingramcontent.com/pod-product-compliance
Lightning Source LLC
Chambersburg PA
CBHW080851170526
45158CB00009B/2704